INSPIRING SPORTS STORIES FOR KIDS

Fun, Inspirational Facts & Stories For Young Readers

FALCON FOCUS

Contents

Introduction ... v

1. The Miracle on Grass: 1980 US Olympic Baseball Team ... 1
2. Babe Ruth's Inspiring Journey ... 7
3. Sarah Fuller's Historic Kick ... 13
4. Tom Brady: The Sixth Round Pick ... 21
5. Bobby Orr's Revolutionary Play as a Defenseman ... 32
6. The Development of the National Women's Hockey League (NWHL) ... 38
7. LeBron James: From High School Phenom to NBA Superstar ... 45
8. The Legend of Michael Jordan ... 52
9. Cristiano Ronaldo's Work Ethic ... 59
10. Lionel Messi's Perseverance ... 68

References ... 77
Bonus: Free Book! ... 79

Copyright © 2023 Falcon Focus

All rights reserved. No part of this publication may be reproduced, distributed or transmitted in any form or by any means, including photocopying, recording, or other electronic or mechanical methods, without the prior written permission of the publisher, except in the case of brief quotations embodied in critical reviews and certain other non-commercial uses permitted by copyright law.

Trademarked names appear throughout this book. Rather than use a trademark symbol with every occurrence of a trademarked name, names are used in an editorial fashion, with no intention of infringement of the respective owner's trademark. The information in this book is distributed on an "as is" basis, without warranty. Although every precaution has been taken in the preparation of this work, neither the author nor the publisher shall have any liability to any person or entity with respect to any loss or damage caused or alleged to be caused directly or indirectly by the information contained in this book.

Introduction

Step into the world of *Inspiring Sports Stories For Kids*, a compilation that will transport you across the diverse landscape of sports, unveiling tales of resilience, determination, and unwavering passion. In this edition, witness the extraordinary impact of athletes who have become beacons of inspiration in their respective sports.

In the Miracle on Grass, we revisit the 1980 US Olympic Baseball Team's extraordinary journey, reminding us that with determination, even the improbable becomes possible. Babe Ruth's Inspiring Journey takes us back in time to discover the origins of a baseball legend, showcasing how resilience and passion can fuel greatness.

Sarah Fuller's historic kick brings a modern touch to our compilation, celebrating the triumph of the first woman to score in a Power Five college football game. Meanwhile, Tom Brady's story, from a sixth-round pick to a football icon, teaches invaluable lessons about perseverance and self-belief.

Bobby Orr's revolutionary play as a defenseman introduces the world of hockey, demonstrating how innovative approaches can redefine a sport. We explore the Development of the National Women's Hockey League (NWHL), shedding light on the growth of women's hockey at the professional level.

Follow in the footsteps of basketball legends Michael Jordan and LeBron James, as they transition from high school phenoms to NBA superstars. Their awe-inspiring journeys unveil the path to success, proving that passion, talent, and hard work are the keys to greatness in the world of basketball.

Finally, turn the pages to explore Cristiano Ronaldo's work ethic, alongside Lionel Messi's perseverance, delving into the dedication and determination that have propelled these soccer superstars to global stardom.

These stories go beyond the scores and statistics, illuminating the human spirit and dedication that make sports an incredible journey. Join me on this exploration through the triumphs, challenges, and enduring legacies of these extraordinary athletes. May these inspiring narratives within these pages ignite a lifelong love for sports and instill the belief that, with dedication and passion, anyone can become a legend in their chosen field.

The Miracle on Grass: 1980 US Olympic Baseball Team

Background and Team Formation

The story of the 1980 US Olympic Baseball Team, often referred to as "The Miracle on Grass," is a captivating tale of underdog triumph and national pride. This team's journey to the 1980 Olympics in Moscow was marked by unexpected challenges and extraordinary achievements. The squad was composed predominantly of amateur and collegiate players, a stark contrast to the professional, seasoned athletes they would face in the international arena. This unique mix of young talents from various universities and amateur clubs across the United States brought a fresh and dynamic approach to the team.

The formation of the 1980 Olympic team was a meticulous process, guided by the goal of assembling a group of players who could not only compete at an international level but also embody the spirit and determination of American baseball. The team's roster included promising college players, some of whom would later achieve significant success in Major League Baseball. This blend of youthful enthusiasm and raw talent was seen as both a strength and a vulnerability, as the team lacked the experience of playing together and facing international competition.

The team's preparation for the Olympics was an intensive period of training and team-building. Coaches focused on honing the skills of these young players, developing strategies that would leverage their strengths against the more experienced international teams. The players underwent rigorous training sessions, which included not only physical conditioning and skill development but also lessons on the nuances of international play, which differed in some respects from American baseball.

As the team came together, a sense of camaraderie and shared purpose began to develop among the players. Despite their diverse backgrounds and limited experience playing as a unit, they shared a common goal: to represent their country on the world stage and challenge the dominant international teams. This unity and determination would become the defining characteristics of the 1980 US Olympic Baseball Team, setting the stage for what would become one of the most remarkable stories in the history of Olympic baseball.

Underdog Status

The 1980 US Olympic Baseball Team's underdog status was a significant aspect of their narrative, particularly in the context of their competition against the Soviet Union team. The Soviet team, composed of seasoned and professionally trained athletes, was seen as a formidable opponent. They had the advantage of extensive experience in international play, a well-established baseball program, and were competing on their home turf, factors that contributed to their perception as the overwhelming favorites. In contrast, the US team, with its roster of amateur and collegiate players, lacked the depth of international experience and the kind of rigorous, specialized training that their Soviet counterparts had received.

This contrast in experience and preparation set the stage for what many viewed as a lopsided contest. The American team's relative inexperience in international competition and their youth were seen as major disadvantages. However, what the US team lacked in experience, they made up for with raw talent, enthusiasm, and a strong desire to prove themselves on the global stage. Their underdog status became a unifying force for the team, fueling their determination to defy expectations and make a mark in the Olympics.

The perception of the US team as underdogs was not just a reflection of their inexperience but also of the broader context of the Cold War. The political tensions between the United States and the Soviet Union added a layer of intensity to the competition, making the baseball field an extension of the larger geopolitical struggle. This backdrop added to the pressure on the young American team, as their performance was seen as more than just a sporting endeavor; it was a representation of national pride and resilience in the face of a powerful adversary.

Despite the odds stacked against them, the US team approached the competition with a positive mindset and a focus on teamwork and strategic play. Their underdog status allowed them to enter the tournament with a sense of freedom and a nothing-to-lose attitude, which proved to be advantageous. The team's journey through the tournament showcased their growing confidence and skill, challenging the preconceived notions of their capabilities and setting the stage for what would become a legendary performance in the annals of Olympic baseball.

Key Moments of the Game

The 1980 US Olympic Baseball Team's journey was marked by several key moments and pivotal plays that culminated in their unexpected victory, particularly in their games against the Soviet Union team. Each game was a tapestry of strategic plays, individual brilliance, and collective effort, with certain moments standing out as turning points in their path to victory. One such moment was a crucial home run hit by a relatively unknown player, which not only boosted the team's morale but also sent a clear message to their opponents about the American team's capability and resolve.

Another significant play was a masterful pitching performance by one of the team's starters. Against a backdrop of high pressure and expectations, this pitcher delivered an exceptional game, striking out several key players from the Soviet team. His performance not only silenced skeptics but also galvanized the American team, reinforcing their belief in their ability to compete against more experienced teams.

Defensive plays were equally pivotal in the US team's success. There were instances of remarkable fielding, including a game-saving catch in the outfield and a critical double play that thwarted a potential rally by the Soviet team. These defensive masterstrokes were not just displays of athletic prowess but also strategic triumphs, showcasing the team's ability to stay calm and focused under pressure.

The team's batting lineup also had its moments of brilliance, with several players contributing to key hits that drove in crucial runs. The collective effort of the team's batters, working in tandem to build pressure on the Soviet pitchers, demonstrated their strategic acumen and adaptability. These batting performances, particularly in clutch situations, were instrumental in swinging the momentum in favor of the American team.

The culmination of these key moments was not just in the individual plays but in how they came together to form a narrative of resilience, teamwork, and the triumph of the underdog. The US team's journey through these games was a series of challenges turned into opportunities, each play building on the last to create a story that resonated far beyond the baseball field. Their victory, achieved through a combination of skill, strategy, and sheer determination, became a defining moment in Olympic baseball history, leaving a lasting impression on all who witnessed it.

Significance of the Win

The victory of the 1980 US Olympic Baseball Team held profound significance not only for the sport of baseball but also for the Olympic Games and the nation as a whole. This win was more than just a triumph in a sports tournament; it represented a remarkable achievement against overwhelming odds and became a source of inspiration and national pride. The success of this young, inexperienced team in a global arena like the Olympics served as a powerful testament to the spirit of perseverance and the potential of teamwork.

In the realm of baseball, the team's victory was a defining moment that highlighted the depth of talent in American baseball, extending beyond the professional leagues. It demonstrated that with the right mix of skill, dedication, and leadership, even a team with less experience could achieve greatness on the world stage. This win contributed significantly to raising the profile of baseball in the Olympics, showcasing the sport's global appeal and competitiveness.

For the Olympic Games, the American team's success was a testament to the ethos of the Olympics – bringing together athletes from diverse backgrounds to compete on a level playing field. It reinforced the idea that the Olympics were not just about winning medals but also about celebrating the human spirit, sportsmanship, and the unifying power of sports. The US team's victory was a story of underdogs triumphing, a narrative that resonates deeply with the Olympic ideals.

Nationally, the victory came at a time when the United States needed a boost of morale. The team's unexpected success provided a sense of joy and pride to Americans, serving as a reminder of the country's resilience and capability. The players, with their diverse backgrounds and humble beginnings, represented the quintessential American spirit of hard work and determination. Their win was a source of inspiration for young athletes and non-athletes alike, demonstrating that with passion and perseverance, any challenge can be overcome and any dream can be achieved.

The legacy of this victory continued to inspire future generations of athletes and sports enthusiasts. The story of the 1980 US Olympic Baseball Team became a cherished part of American sports history, a narrative that spoke to the heart of what it means to strive against the odds, to work as a team, and to achieve something greater than the sum of individual efforts. This remarkable win left an indelible mark on the sports world, reminding everyone of the power of sports to unite, inspire, and celebrate human achievement.

Babe Ruth's Inspiring Journey

Challenging Childhood

Babe Ruth's journey to becoming one of baseball's greatest legends began with a challenging childhood in Baltimore, Maryland. Born George Herman Ruth Jr. in 1895, Ruth faced a tumultuous early life that significantly influenced his path to baseball stardom. His childhood was marked by poverty and hardship, growing up in a rough neighborhood where survival often took precedence over schooling and childhood play.

Ruth's parents, struggling to make ends meet and manage their large family, found it increasingly difficult to control their son's rebellious behavior. This led to his placement at St. Mary's Industrial School for Boys, a reformatory and orphanage, at the age of seven. The strict discipline and regimented structure of St. Mary's were a stark contrast to the freedom and chaos of his life in Baltimore's streets. However, it was at St. Mary's that Ruth found his refuge and calling in baseball.

At St. Mary's, Ruth was under the guidance of Brother Matthias Boutlier, a disciplinarian yet caring figure who introduced him to baseball. Brother Matthias recognized Ruth's natural talent for the game and became his mentor, nurturing his abilities as a player. Ruth quickly excelled in baseball, showing an early aptitude for both pitching and batting. The sport provided a positive outlet for his energy and a focus for his ambitions, setting him on a path that would lead him away from the hardships of his early life.

Ruth's time at St. Mary's was more than just an escape from his troubled upbringing; it was a foundational period that shaped his future. The discipline he learned at the school, combined with the baseball skills he developed, prepared him for the challenges and opportunities that lay ahead. This period of his life instilled in him the perseverance, determination, and passion for baseball that would become the hallmarks of his legendary career. Ruth's challenging childhood and the transformative years at St. Mary's Industrial School for Boys were crucial in molding the young boy into the sports icon he would eventually become.

Rise to Stardom

Babe Ruth's rise to stardom in professional baseball is a story of extraordinary talent and transformation. His journey to becoming one of the most iconic figures in the sport began with his entry into professional baseball, which was marked by an early demonstration of his remarkable skills. Ruth started his professional career as a pitcher for the Baltimore Orioles of the International League, where his abilities on the mound quickly garnered attention. However, it was his move to the Boston Red Sox in 1914 that marked the beginning of his rise in Major League Baseball.

With the Red Sox, Ruth's talents as a pitcher flourished. He was known for his powerful left arm, delivering pitches with speed and accuracy that made him one of the top pitchers in the league. His pitching prowess helped lead the Red Sox to three World Series titles in 1915, 1916, and 1918. Despite his success as a pitcher, it was Ruth's potential at the plate that set him apart. He began to show an exceptional ability for hitting, which would eventually lead to a dramatic shift in his baseball career.

Ruth's transformation into a legendary hitter began in earnest with his move to the New York Yankees in 1920. This change marked a significant turning point in his career and the sport of baseball. With the Yankees, Ruth transitioned from being a pitcher to an outfielder, allowing him to focus more on batting. His impact as a hitter was immediate and profound. Ruth's home runs were not just frequent; they were majestic, often traveling extraordinary distances. His ability to hit home runs changed the way the game was played, making it more exciting and drawing more fans to the sport.

Ruth's time with the Yankees saw him shatter multiple batting records, including the most home runs in a single season and the most career home runs. His charisma and larger-than-life personality, combined with his unprecedented skills at the plate, made him a national celebrity. Ruth's rise to stardom was not just about his transformation from a pitcher to a hitter; it was about revolutionizing baseball, making it a sport of power and spectacle. His entry into professional baseball and subsequent success with the Boston Red Sox and transformation with the New York Yankees is a testament to his unparalleled talent and enduring impact on the sport.

Record-Breaking Achievements

Babe Ruth's career in baseball is synonymous with record-breaking achievements, particularly in the realm of home run hitting. His impact on the game and the New York Yankees was monumental, changing the nature of baseball and capturing the imagination of fans across the nation. Ruth's ability to hit home runs with stunning frequency and distance transformed him into a baseball legend and altered the way the game was played and perceived.

Ruth's home run records are a cornerstone of his legacy. In 1920, his first year with the Yankees, he hit a staggering 54 home runs, more than any other team in the American League that year. This feat was not a one-off occurrence; Ruth consistently led the league in home runs, including hitting a then-unprecedented 60 home runs in the 1927 season. This record stood for 34 years, evidence of Ruth's extraordinary power at the plate. His career total of 714 home runs was a record that remained unbroken for decades, underscoring his dominance in this aspect of the game.

Beyond his individual records, Ruth's impact on the New York Yankees' successes was profound. He helped the team win seven American League pennants and four World Series titles. His presence in the lineup made the Yankees a formidable team, feared by pitchers and admired by fans. Ruth's ability to draw crowds and generate excitement about the game contributed significantly to the team's financial success and popularity.

Ruth's influence extended beyond his statistical achievements; he changed the game of baseball itself. Before Ruth, baseball was largely a game of strategy, focused on bunting, stealing bases, and singles. Ruth introduced the concept of power-hitting, making home runs a central and thrilling part of the game. His style of play captivated fans and inspired future generations of players, shifting the focus of baseball from a low-scoring, strategic game to one characterized by power and excitement.

Babe Ruth's record-breaking achievements in home run hitting and his impact on the Yankees and baseball as a whole are integral to his enduring legacy. He transformed the sport with his exceptional talent, reshaping baseball into America's beloved pastime. Ruth's influence on the game is still felt today, and his records and approach to baseball continue to be a benchmark and inspiration in the sport.

Off-Field Impact and Legacy

Babe Ruth's influence extended well beyond the baseball diamond, characterized by his larger-than-life personality and his significant charitable endeavors. Off the field, Ruth was known for his charismatic and gregarious nature, which endeared him to fans and made him a cultural icon of his time. His love for the game and joyous approach to life resonated with the public, making him one of the most beloved figures in the history of American sports.

Ruth's charitable work was a significant aspect of his off-field activities. He had a soft spot for children, often visiting hospitals and orphanages, where he would spend time with young fans. Ruth's generosity was not just limited to his time; he was also known for his financial contributions to various charities and causes. His involvement in charity work was driven by a deep sense of empathy and a desire to give back to the community, particularly to those less fortunate.

Beyond his charitable actions, Ruth's legacy as a public figure was marked by the way he handled fame. Despite his superstar status, he remained approachable and relatable, often interacting with fans and the media in a candid and jovial manner. This accessibility and genuine nature contributed significantly to his popularity and enduring legacy.

Ruth's legacy as one of baseball's greatest icons is undisputed. He revolutionized the sport with his extraordinary skills and changed how it was played and perceived. His name became synonymous with baseball greatness, inspiring future generations of players and fans alike. Ruth's impact on the game of baseball and American culture was profound, making him not just a sports hero but also a cultural icon.

Babe Ruth's off-field impact, combined with his unparalleled achievements in baseball, cemented his status as a legend in the truest sense. His enduring legacy is evident in the continued admiration and reverence he receives, decades after his passing. Ruth's larger-than-life personality, his charitable endeavors, and his contributions to baseball have ensured that his memory lives on, not just as a phenomenal athlete but as a symbol of joy, generosity, and the enduring spirit of America's pastime.

Sarah Fuller's Historic Kick

Background

Sarah Fuller's historic journey to a groundbreaking moment in football began with her career in another sport: soccer. Fuller's background as a soccer player laid the foundation for her eventual transition into football history, showcasing her athletic skills and pioneering spirit.

Born on June 20, 1999, in Wylie, Texas, Fuller grew up with a passion for soccer, dedicating herself to the sport from a young age. Her talent and hard work in soccer led her to play at the collegiate level, where she became a key player for the Vanderbilt University women's soccer team. As a goalkeeper for Vanderbilt, Fuller demonstrated remarkable skills, including agility, strong decision-making, and leadership on the field. These qualities were pivotal in her soccer career and would later become instrumental in her historic transition to football.

During her time with the Vanderbilt soccer team, Fuller was known for her competitiveness and work ethic. She played an integral role in the team's defense, consistently delivering performances that helped secure victories and uphold the team's competitive standing. Her ability to perform under pressure and maintain composure in high-stakes situations was a testament to her athletic prowess and mental toughness.

Fuller's success in soccer was marked by team achievements and personal accolades, reflecting her impact as a player. She was part of a Vanderbilt team that made significant strides in collegiate soccer, contributing to its defensive strength. Her leadership qualities were also recognized by her teammates and coaches, as she often stepped up in crucial moments to guide and motivate the team.

Transition to Football

In the fall of 2020, the Vanderbilt football team found itself in a challenging situation due to the COVID-19 pandemic. Several of the team's specialists, including kickers, were unavailable for a game against the Missouri Tigers due to COVID-19 protocols. This situation led the football team's coaching staff to look for alternatives within the university's athletic programs.

Aware of Fuller's accomplishments as a goalkeeper for the Vanderbilt women's soccer team, the football coaches recognized potential in her strong kicking ability. They approached Fuller with the opportunity to join the football team as a kicker. Fuller, fresh off her participation in the SEC Championship with the soccer team, accepted the offer, seeing it as a chance to contribute to another Vanderbilt sports team and embrace a new athletic challenge.

Fuller's decision to join the football team was a significant one, not just for her but for the sport of football. By agreeing to play as a kicker, she was set to break barriers in an overwhelmingly male-dominated sport. Her willingness to step into this new role demonstrated her courage and commitment to pushing boundaries in collegiate sports.

Fuller's transition to football involved a rapid adjustment period. She had to acclimate to the different techniques and dynamics of football kicking, as opposed to soccer goalkeeping. Her practice sessions with the football team were focused on honing her skills for kickoffs and point-after attempts, translating her soccer skills into football proficiency.

The Historic Game

Sarah Fuller's historic moment in football occurred on November 28, 2020, during a game that would etch her name in the annals of sports history. This game, where she took to the field as a kicker for the Vanderbilt University football team, marked a groundbreaking moment in the traditionally male-dominated sport of college football.

The game was an SEC matchup between Vanderbilt and the University of Missouri. Held at Memorial Stadium in Columbia, Missouri, the game drew significant attention, not just for the competition itself, but for the anticipation of Fuller's participation. Her presence on the roster had made national headlines, sparking conversations about gender barriers in sports.

Fuller's opportunity came on November 28, after halftime. Vanderbilt, trailing in the game, turned to Fuller to execute the second-half kickoff. This moment was laden with significance, as it marked the first time a woman played in a Power Five conference football game, the highest level of college football in the United States.

Dressed in Vanderbilt gear with the words "Play Like a Girl" on the back of her helmet, a nod to the slogan promoting female participation in sports, Fuller approached the kickoff with confidence. She executed a perfectly-placed squib kick that was downed by Missouri at their 35-yard line, ensuring no return. While the kick was tactically planned, it was also symbolic, representing a barrier-breaking moment in the sport.

Fuller's historic play was met with widespread recognition and celebration. Her teammates and coaches, along with the spectators, acknowledged the significance of the moment. The impact of her participation transcended the game's score or outcome, marking a milestone for gender inclusion and diversity in sports.

Her participation in this game was not only a personal achievement for Fuller but also a monumental step forward for women in sports. It challenged long-standing gender norms and inspired countless young girls and women, demonstrating that opportunities in sports should not be limited by gender.

Challenges and Reaction

One of the primary challenges Fuller faced was the physical and technical transition from soccer to football. Kicking a football, especially in a game situation, required adapting her soccer skills to the nuances of football, a challenge she embraced with determination. Additionally, the intense scrutiny and pressure that came with being in the national spotlight presented a mental and emotional challenge. Fuller had to navigate this while staying focused on her performance.

There was also the challenge of entering a male-dominated sport, where female participation at this level was unprecedented. Fuller had to integrate into the team and adapt to a new sporting environment, all under the watchful eyes of the media and the public. This situation required not only physical skill and mental toughness but also a strong sense of self-confidence and resilience.

The public reaction to Fuller's participation was mixed, though largely positive and supportive. Many people, including prominent figures in sports and other fields, praised her for breaking barriers and setting an example for young girls and women. Her appearance was seen as a significant step forward for gender equality in sports, inspiring countless aspiring female athletes.

However, Fuller's role as a trailblazer also attracted criticism and skepticism from some quarters. Critics questioned the quality of her play and the motives behind her inclusion on the team. This criticism was part of the broader discourse about the place of women in traditionally male-dominated sports.

Fuller's teammates and the Vanderbilt community largely supported her. They recognized the courage and commitment it took for her to step into this new role and appreciated the attention and conversation her participation brought to the team and the university.

Additionally, Fuller's achievement sparked discussions in the wider sports community about opportunities for women in sports, challenging traditional gender norms and highlighting the need for greater inclusivity. Her historic kick was not just a personal achievement but a moment that prompted reflection on the progress and potential in women's sports.

Gender Barriers in Sports

Fuller's accomplishment is particularly noteworthy considering the landscape of college football, a sport that has traditionally been an exclusively male domain, especially at the Power Five conference level. Her presence on the field challenged the preconceived notions about the roles and capabilities of female athletes in such a high-profile and physically demanding sport. It sent a powerful message that skill and talent are not confined by gender.

The significance of Fuller's achievement extends beyond her personal accomplishment; it symbolizes the broader struggle for gender equality in sports. Her participation in a college football game highlighted the disparities that still exist in athletic opportunities and recognition between men and women. It brought to light the ongoing need to advocate for equal opportunities for female athletes in all sports, including those traditionally dominated by men.

Fuller's role in breaking gender barriers also served as an inspiration for young girls and women with aspirations in sports, demonstrating that the boundaries of what is possible are continually expanding. Her story is a vivid example that can encourage young female athletes to pursue their sporting ambitions, even in fields where they may be underrepresented.

Furthermore, her achievement prompted discussions about how sports organizations, from youth leagues to professional levels, can create more inclusive environments. It underscored the importance of providing support systems, resources, and equitable opportunities for female athletes. Fuller's participation in a football game is a reminder of the need for ongoing advocacy and action to ensure that gender does not limit access to sports and athletic development.

In the larger societal context, Fuller's historic kick resonates beyond the realm of sports, contributing to the dialogue about gender roles and equality in various sectors. It illustrates how sports can be a catalyst for social change and a platform for challenging stereotypes and advocating for equality.

Role Model and Inspiration

Sarah Fuller's story transcends the realm of sports, positioning her as a role model and source of inspiration for young girls and boys alike. Her groundbreaking achievement in college football exemplifies qualities such as courage, perseverance, and the willingness to challenge norms, making her an influential figure for the younger generation.

For young girls, Fuller's journey is a powerful illustration of breaking gender barriers and challenging societal expectations. Her success in a male-dominated sport provides tangible proof that girls can aspire to and achieve greatness in any field they choose, regardless of traditional gender roles. Fuller's story sends a message of empowerment, encouraging young girls to pursue their passions and dreams with confidence, even in areas where they may be underrepresented.

Boys, too, can draw inspiration from Fuller's story. It teaches them the importance of inclusivity and respect for diversity in all aspects of life, including sports. Seeing a woman excel in a role traditionally held by men can help young boys understand and appreciate the value of equality and the need to support and celebrate achievements irrespective of gender. Fuller's story can contribute to shaping a more equitable mindset in boys from a young age.

Moreover, Fuller's embodiment of resilience and determination in the face of challenges is a universal lesson. Her ability to step into a high-pressure situation, adapt to a new environment, and perform with composure is inspirational for all young people. It underscores the virtues of hard work, dedication, and staying focused on one's goals, regardless of the obstacles.

Fuller also represents the importance of seizing opportunities and being open to new experiences. Her willingness to take on a challenge outside her comfort zone is a valuable lesson in personal growth and exploration. This aspect of her story encourages young people to be open-minded and courageous in exploring their own potential and interests.

In addition to her achievements on the field, Fuller's positive attitude, team spirit, and advocacy for inclusivity make her a role model off the field. Her engagement with initiatives like "Play Like a Girl" and her advocacy for female participation in sports serve as further inspiration, highlighting her commitment to making a difference beyond her athletic accomplishments.

Sarah Fuller's role as a model and inspiration is significant for young girls and boys. Her story is a compelling example of challenging gender norms, demonstrating resilience, and embracing opportunities. It inspires young people to pursue their dreams with determination and confidence, promotes inclusivity and equality, and highlights the importance of hard work and a positive attitude in achieving one's goals.

Tom Brady: The Sixth Round Pick

Early Career and Draft

Tom Brady's journey to becoming one of the greatest quarterbacks in NFL history is a remarkable tale of perseverance and belief in oneself, beginning with an often overlooked and undervalued start. Born on August 3, 1977, in San Mateo, California, Brady nurtured his passion for football from a young age, idolizing players like Joe Montana and dreaming of one day playing in the NFL. His early years were marked by a deep dedication to the sport, playing as a quarterback for Junipero Serra High School in San Mateo.

Despite his early passion and commitment, Brady was not a standout star in high school. He was good, but not exceptional in the eyes of many college scouts. His journey to the University of Michigan as a quarterback was the first step in a career characterized by patience and resilience. At Michigan, Brady found himself seventh on the depth chart and struggled to get playing time. However, his determination never waned. He spent hours studying game films, working on his technique, and preparing mentally and physically for the opportunity to lead his team. By his junior year, he had fought his way up to be the starting quarterback.

Brady's college career was marked by significant improvement and moments of brilliance, yet doubts persisted among NFL scouts. His NFL Combine performance in 2000 did little to quell these doubts. He was not particularly fast, his arm strength was questioned, and his physical build was deemed less than ideal for an NFL quarterback. These factors contributed to Brady being largely overlooked in the 2000 NFL Draft.

As the draft progressed, Brady watched as quarterback after quarterback was chosen ahead of him. The experience was emotionally taxing. He later recounted the disappointment and frustration he felt as he waited for his name to be called, a wait that seemed endless and disheartening. In an interview, Brady shared how he stepped outside his family's house, fighting back tears, trying to come to terms with the uncertainty of his football future.

Finally, in the sixth round, with the 199th overall pick, the New England Patriots selected Tom Brady. This selection was not celebrated with great fanfare. Few could have predicted that this sixth-round pick would go on to redefine success in the NFL. For Brady, it was both a relief and a new beginning, a chance to prove his worth in a league that had largely undervalued his potential.

The draft experience instilled in Brady a chip on his shoulder, a relentless drive to prove not just to the world, but to himself, that he was more than just a sixth-round pick. It was this drive, born from the uncertainty and disappointment of his draft experience, that would fuel his legendary NFL career.

Consistency and Durability

Upon joining the New England Patriots, Brady quickly began to demonstrate his unwavering commitment to the game. He embraced a rigorous fitness and nutrition regimen, one that he would refine and adhere to throughout his career. This dedication to his physical well-being was a key factor in his remarkable longevity in the league. Brady's approach went beyond traditional training methods; he focused on pliability, nutrition, hydration, and mental training, which helped him stay at the top of his game well into his 40s, a rare feat in the physically demanding world of professional football.

Brady's record for consecutive starts is a testament to his durability. He began his starting role in the 2001 season, after an injury to then-starter Drew Bledsoe. From that moment, Brady seized the opportunity and never looked back. He led the Patriots to their first Super Bowl victory that season and established himself as an irreplaceable asset to the team. His ability to consistently perform at a high level, game after game, season after season, set him apart from his peers.

One of the most significant aspects of Brady's career has been his ability to avoid serious injury. Apart from the 2008 season, when he suffered a knee injury in the opening game and missed the  remainder of the season, Brady has been remarkably injury-free. This is no small feat in the NFL, where the physical toll on players, especially quarterbacks, is immense. Brady's commitment to his off-season and in-season training played a crucial role in this. He worked tirelessly on strengthening his body, understanding that durability was just as important as skill in ensuring a long and successful career.

Furthermore, Brady's mental toughness and ability to perform under pressure contributed greatly to his consistency. He was known for his cool demeanor in high-stress situations, often leading his team to victory in the final minutes of the game. This mental fortitude, combined with his physical preparedness, made him one of the most reliable players in the league.

Over the years, Brady's consistency has been a cornerstone of the Patriots' dynasty. He led the team to nine Super Bowl appearances, winning six of them. His longevity and consistent high-level performance are unparalleled, earning him the respect of teammates, coaches, and opponents alike.

In an era where player movement is common, and careers can be cut short by injury, Brady's consistency and durability stand as a shining example. He redefined what it means to be a quarterback in the NFL, not just through his skill and leadership but through his extraordinary ability to remain at the peak of his game for over two decades.

Challenges and Resilience

Tom Brady's journey to becoming one of the greatest quarterbacks in NFL history was not without its fair share of challenges. From internal competition within his team to widespread public skepticism, Brady faced numerous obstacles that tested his resilience and determination.

When Brady joined the New England Patriots, he was not immediately seen as a star player. He started as the fourth-string quarterback and had to work tirelessly to prove himself. The competition within the team was intense. Brady was up against established players, including Drew Bledsoe, a highly regarded and well-established quarterback. The challenge for Brady was not just to match the physical skills of his competitors but to demonstrate a unique value that he could bring to the team.

Brady's opportunity came in the 2001 season when Bledsoe was injured. Brady stepped in and quickly proved his worth, leading the team to victory after victory. However, even with this success, there were doubts about whether he could sustain this level of performance. The initial view of many was that Brady was a temporary solution, a stop-gap until Bledsoe returned. Yet, Brady continued to excel, turning skepticism into admiration and eventually becoming the team's undisputed starting quarterback.

Another significant challenge Brady faced was public skepticism. Early in his career, he was often viewed as a system quarterback, one who succeeded due to the Patriots' system rather than his own abilities. This perception was fueled by the team's continued success, regardless of the individual players in the lineup. Brady had to constantly prove that his success was not just a product of the system but a result of his skill, intelligence, and hard work.

The "Deflategate" scandal was another challenge that tested Brady's resilience. He faced accusations of having knowingly used under-inflated footballs in the 2015 AFC Championship Game against the Indianapolis Colts. This controversy led to a four-game suspension at the start of the 2016 season. The incident was a significant challenge to Brady's reputation and legacy. However, he responded by maintaining his innocence, staying focused on the game, and returning to lead the Patriots to another Super Bowl victory in the same season.

Throughout his career, Brady also faced the challenge of evolving with the game and adapting to new team dynamics as players and coaches came and went. His ability to continually adjust his style of play to fit new strategies and teammates showcased not only his physical ability but also his mental acuity and adaptability.

Brady's resilience in the face of these challenges is a key part of his legacy. He did not allow competition, skepticism, or controversy to derail his focus or commitment to the sport.

Instead, he used these challenges as fuel to further enhance his performance and cement his status as one of the greatest quarterbacks in NFL history.

Achievements

Tom Brady's list of achievements and accolades is extensive, marking him as one of the most accomplished players in NFL history. His career is studded with remarkable milestones, from Super Bowl victories to numerous NFL records.

Brady's most notable achievements are his seven Super Bowl victories, the most by any player in NFL history. These wins came in Super Bowls XXXVI, XXXVIII, XXXIX, XLIX, LI, LIII, and LV. Each victory highlighted different stages of Brady's career and showcased his ability to lead his team to success under varying circumstances.

- Super Bowl XXXVI (2002): Brady's first Super Bowl win came against the St. Louis Rams. Then a young quarterback, he led a game-winning drive in the final minutes, beginning his legacy as a clutch performer.
- Super Bowl XXXVIII (2004) and XXXIX (2005): These consecutive wins against the Carolina Panthers and Philadelphia Eagles solidified the Patriots' status as a dynasty and Brady's reputation as an elite quarterback.
- Super Bowl XLIX (2015): Against the Seattle Seahawks, Brady orchestrated another late-game comeback, further cementing his legacy.
- Super Bowl LI (2017): Perhaps his most remarkable Super Bowl performance, Brady led the Patriots to overcome a 28-3 deficit against the Atlanta Falcons, the largest comeback in Super Bowl history.

- Super Bowl LIII (2019): A win against the Los Angeles Rams, this victory was a testament to Brady's longevity and sustained excellence.
- Super Bowl LV (2021): Winning with the Tampa Bay Buccaneers, Brady proved his ability to achieve the pinnacle of success outside of the New England Patriots' system.

In addition to his Super Bowl victories, Brady has numerous NFL records. Some of his most significant records include:

- Brady holds the record for the most career wins by an NFL quarterback.
- He has thrown more touchdown passes than any other quarterback in NFL history.
- Brady has amassed the most passing yards in NFL history.

Brady has also been recognized with numerous individual awards. He is a three-time NFL Most Valuable Player (MVP), awarded in 2007, 2010, and 2017. He has been selected to 14 Pro Bowls, showcasing his consistent high-level performance over two decades.

Moreover, Brady's achievements extend beyond these statistics and accolades. He has set numerous playoff records, including most games played, most games won, and most touchdown passes. His postseason success is a significant part of his legacy, demonstrating his ability to perform at his best when the stakes are highest.

Work Ethic and Leadership

Tom Brady's exceptional work ethic and leadership have been central to his sustained success and the success of his teams.

These qualities have not only defined his personal career but have also significantly impacted the culture and performance of every team he has been part of.

Brady's approach to preparation and training is legendary. He is known for being the first to arrive and the last to leave during training sessions, setting a standard for commitment and dedication. His meticulous attention to detail in studying game film, understanding opponents' strategies, and mastering the Patriots' and later the Buccaneers' playbooks, became a hallmark of his career. This relentless pursuit of excellence extended to his physical training and nutrition. Brady adopted a holistic approach to his health, integrating strict dietary plans and innovative training methods that focused on flexibility and longevity, rather than just strength and endurance. This approach not only prolonged his career but also served as a model for younger players.

Brady's mental preparation is as rigorous as his physical training. He spent countless hours studying the game, understanding the nuances, and preparing for every possible scenario. This level of preparation ensured that he was seldom caught off-guard on the field and could make rapid, intelligent decisions under pressure.

Beyond his personal preparation, Brady's leadership style significantly influenced his teams. He led by example, demonstrating what dedication and focus looked like. His ability to remain calm under pressure, maintain a positive attitude, and rally his team in tough situations was inspirational. Brady was not just a leader in terms of gameplay; he was a mentor to younger players, sharing his knowledge and experience and fostering a supportive team environment.

Brady's influence extended to the entire team culture. His high standards and commitment to excellence raised the bar for everyone around him. Teammates often spoke of how Brady's presence motivated them to work harder and perform better.

This influence was particularly evident during critical moments in games, where Brady's composure and confidence had a calming effect on his teammates, enabling them to focus and perform at their best.

Brady's ability to adapt his leadership style to different teammates and situations was another key aspect of his success. Whether it was connecting with veteran players or guiding rookies, he knew how to communicate effectively and build strong relationships. This adaptability was crucial when he moved from the New England Patriots to the Tampa Bay Buccaneers, where he successfully integrated into a new team and led them to a Super Bowl victory.

Tom Brady's work ethic and leadership were not just about setting personal records; they were about elevating the performance and mindset of his entire team. He instilled a culture of excellence, commitment, and resilience, which became the cornerstone of his teams' successes.

Legacy

Brady's influence on the sport of American football extends far beyond his impressive array of records and accolades. His legacy is one that has reshaped the narrative of what it means to be a successful athlete in the NFL and has provided invaluable lessons for young players aspiring to greatness.

Brady's career has redefined the quarterback role, showing that success at the position requires more than just physical skills. He demonstrated that mental acuity, game management, adaptability, and leadership are equally important. His ability to read defenses, adjust plays at the line of scrimmage, and maintain composure under pressure set new standards for quarterback performance.

Brady's success and longevity have had a profound impact on how teams view the quarterback position and the draft process. He challenged the notion that only high draft picks can become elite quarterbacks, showing that determination, work ethic, and continuous improvement are critical to success. His career has inspired teams to look beyond traditional metrics and consider the intangible qualities that contribute to a player's success.

Brady became a cultural icon, transcending the sport. His commitment to excellence and his personal story of overcoming odds have inspired countless fans and players. He has shown that with perseverance and dedication, it is possible to achieve one's dreams, regardless of where one starts.

Brady's career offers several lessons for young players. Firstly, it emphasizes the importance of a strong work ethic. Brady's dedication to training, preparation, and continual improvement is a blueprint for success. Secondly, it highlights the value of mental toughness and resilience. His ability to bounce back from setbacks, whether it be a poor draft position or on-field challenges, is a testament to his mental strength. Thirdly, Brady's career underscores the significance of adaptability and lifelong learning. He consistently adapted his play style and strategies to suit his team's needs and to stay competitive in a changing league.

Brady's approach to health and fitness, focusing on longevity and injury prevention, has influenced how athletes take care of their bodies. His advocacy for holistic wellness, including diet, mental health, and alternative training methods, has inspired players to consider how off-field habits impact their on-field performance.

Beyond his physical abilities, Brady has been a role model for leadership. His ability to inspire and lead his teammates, to set a high standard for performance, and to maintain a team-first attitude has set an example for what it means to be a leader in a team sport.

Tom Brady's legacy in the NFL is characterized by his transformation from an overlooked draft pick to one of the greatest players in the history of the sport. His career serves as an inspiring example of how dedication, resilience, and a commitment to continuous improvement can lead to extraordinary achievements. For young players, Brady's journey is a lesson in never underestimating the power of hard work, mental fortitude, and the relentless pursuit of one's goals.

Bobby Orr's Revolutionary Play as a Defenseman

Early Career and Entry into the NHL

Bobby Orr's journey to becoming one of the most revolutionary players in hockey history began long before he made his mark with the Boston Bruins. Born on March 20, 1948, in Parry Sound, Ontario, Orr displayed an extraordinary talent for hockey from a young age. Growing up in a small town, Orr honed his skills on local rinks, quickly standing out for his exceptional skating ability and understanding of the game. His early years were characterized by a deep passion for hockey and a work ethic that set him apart from his peers. Orr's talent was evident, and he soon caught the attention of scouts across Canada.

As a teenager, Orr's career took a significant turn when he joined the Oshawa Generals, a junior team in the Ontario Hockey Association. It was here that Orr began to develop the skills and style of play that would later define his career in the NHL. Even at this early stage, Orr's play was revolutionary. As a defenseman, he was not content to limit his role to traditional defensive duties; instead, he actively involved himself in offensive plays, showcasing his remarkable skating and puck-handling skills. This approach to the defenseman position was unconventional at the time, but Orr's success with it was undeniable.

Orr's entry into the NHL came in 1966 when he signed with the Boston Bruins. His debut was highly anticipated, and he did not disappoint. From his first season, Orr's impact on the team was transformative. He brought a new dynamism to the Bruins' defense, contributing significantly to both offensive and defensive plays. His ability to control the game, combined with his speed and agility, made him a standout player from the outset. Orr's innovative style of play began to challenge the traditional perceptions of the role of a defenseman in hockey.

Orr's early years with the Bruins were marked by individual achievements and a clear indication of his potential to change the game. He won the Calder Trophy as the league's best rookie, a sign of the significant impact he was already having in the NHL. Orr's presence on the ice was electrifying, and he quickly became one of the most exciting players to watch. His entry into the NHL and initial years with the Bruins set the stage for what would become a legendary career, marked by unparalleled achievements and a revolutionary approach to the defenseman position. Bobby Orr's early career and entry into the NHL were the beginnings of a journey that would see him redefine the role of a defenseman and leave a lasting legacy in the world of hockey.

Transforming the Defenseman Role

Bobby Orr's transformation of the defenseman role in hockey was nothing short of revolutionary. Prior to Orr's arrival in the

NHL, defensemen were primarily expected to focus on preventing scoring opportunities, with limited involvement in offensive plays. Orr, however, redefined this position with his unique playstyle, blending defensive responsibilities with a strong offensive presence. His approach to the game was characterized by an unparalleled skating ability. Orr's speed and agility on the ice allowed him to move effortlessly between defense and offense, breaking away from traditional defensive roles. His skating wasn't just about speed; it was about control and the ability to maneuver through opponents with ease. This mobility enabled him to support his team's offensive plays while still fulfilling his defensive duties.

Orr's offensive playstyle as a defenseman was groundbreaking. He was not content to simply pass the puck to forwards; instead, he actively participated in creating scoring opportunities. Orr had an exceptional ability to read the game, anticipating plays and making decisive moves that often led to goals or goal opportunities. His skill in handling the puck, combined with his speed, made him a formidable force on the offensive front. He had the rare ability to lead an attack, weaving through opposing players and setting up plays or scoring himself. This offensive contribution from a defenseman was innovative and changed the way the position was played.

Orr's game intelligence was another key factor in his transformation of the defenseman role. He had a deep understanding of the game, allowing him to make smart decisions quickly. Orr could assess situations on the ice with remarkable clarity, knowing when to push forward into an offensive play and when to hang back and focus on defense. His vision of the game was holistic; he understood the importance of positioning, timing, and strategy, both for himself and his team.

Bobby Orr's impact on the defenseman role had a lasting effect on the sport of hockey. He showed that defensemen could be integral to a team's offense without compromising their defensive responsibilities. His style inspired future generations of defensemen to adopt a more dynamic and involved approach to the position. Orr's legacy in transforming the defenseman role is reflected in the way the position is played today, with many defensemen now actively contributing to their team's offensive play, a shift that can be attributed largely to Orr's revolutionary approach to the game.

Career Highlights and Achievements

Bobby Orr's career is adorned with a multitude of highlights and achievements that underscore his status as one of the greatest hockey players of all time. Throughout his career, Orr accumulated an impressive array of awards and records, setting new standards for excellence in the sport. One of Orr's most significant achievements was his collection of Norris Trophies. Awarded annually to the NHL's top defenseman, the Norris Trophy became almost synonymous with Orr during his career. He won the award an unprecedented eight consecutive times from 1968 to 1975, a testament to his dominance in the defenseman role and his all-around excellence on the ice.

In addition to his individual accolades, Orr's contributions to team success were equally remarkable. He was instrumental in leading the Boston Bruins to Stanley Cup victories in 1970 and 1972. Orr's performance in the 1970 Stanley Cup playoffs was particularly memorable, culminating in the iconic overtime goal that clinched the championship for the Bruins. This moment, captured in a famous photograph of Orr flying through the air after scoring, has become one of the most enduring images in hockey history. Orr's impact in the Stanley Cup victories went beyond scoring; he was a key player in all aspects of the game, from defense to creating scoring opportunities.

Orr's record-setting performances extended to various aspects of the game. He was the first defenseman in NHL history to score over 100 points in a season, a feat he achieved three times in his career. His offensive production from the defenseman position was unprecedented, redefining what was considered possible for players in that role. Orr also set the record for most points in a single season by a defenseman, a record that stood for decades. His ability to consistently score and assist while fulfilling defensive responsibilities was unmatched.

Orr's career was not just about the accumulation of awards and records; it was about the way he played the game. His dynamic and skillful style of play brought a new level of excitement to hockey, captivating fans and inspiring future generations of players. Orr's achievements on the ice have left a lasting legacy, securing his place in the annals of hockey history as one of the sport's most exceptional and influential players. His career highlights and achievements are a reflection of his unique talent, his dedication to the sport, and his impact on the game of hockey.

Legacy in Hockey

Bobby Orr's lasting impact on the sport of hockey is immeasurable, transcending his impressive list of achievements and records. Orr revolutionized the role of the defenseman, transforming it from a primarily defensive position into one that is integral to the offensive dynamics of the game. His style of play, characterized by exceptional skating, offensive prowess, and defensive skill, redefined what it meant to be a defenseman. Orr's influence on the sport can be seen in the generations of defensemen who followed him. Many have emulated his style, blending defensive responsibilities with offensive contributions, a testament to Orr's lasting impact on the position. His legacy is evident in the way defensemen are evaluated and utilized in the modern game, with greater emphasis on versatility and offensive ability.

Beyond his technical contributions to the sport, Orr's impact on hockey is also reflected in the way he inspired future generations of players. His exciting, dynamic style of play captivated fans and aspiring hockey players alike, making him a role model for many who took up the sport. Orr's passion for hockey, coupled with his humility and sportsmanship, endeared him to fans and players, making his influence on the sport more than just his on-ice accomplishments. Orr's approach to the game, marked by innovation and excellence, has left a lasting mark on hockey, inspiring players to push the boundaries of their positions and abilities.

Recognized as one of the greatest players in NHL history, Orr's legacy is not confined to the records he set or the trophies he won. It is also about the lasting changes he brought to the game. His impact on hockey is seen in the way the sport has evolved since his playing days, with defensemen now playing a more prominent role in the offensive play of their teams. Orr's legacy in hockey is a blend of his groundbreaking contributions to the sport, his inspirational influence on players and fans, and his status as a hockey icon. His name is synonymous with excellence in hockey, and his legacy continues to be celebrated by those who appreciate the profound impact he had on the sport.

The Development of the National Women's Hockey League (NWHL)

Founding of the NWHL

The National Women's Hockey League (NWHL) was established in 2015, marking a significant milestone in the history of women's sports. It became the first professional women's hockey league in North America to pay its players, heralding a new era of opportunity and recognition for female hockey athletes. The league's formation was a response to the growing demand for a professional platform for women's hockey, a space where female players could showcase their talent and passion for the game at a competitive level. The NWHL's inception was a culmination of years of advocacy, dedication, and hard work by numerous individuals committed to advancing women's hockey.

The league's foundation was driven by the vision of creating a sustainable professional environment for women's hockey. Dani

Rylan, the founder and first commissioner of the NWHL, played a pivotal role in turning this vision into a reality. The goal was to provide female hockey players with opportunities similar to those available to their male counterparts in the NHL. This included not just the chance to play professionally but also to be compensated for their skill and dedication to the sport. The NWHL began with four teams: the Boston Pride, Buffalo Beauts, Connecticut Whale, and New York Riveters (later renamed the Metropolitan Riveters). Each team was located in a market with a strong hockey presence, aiming to tap into the existing fan base and generate local support.

The launch of the NWHL was a significant step forward in promoting women's hockey. It provided a much-needed platform for top female players to continue their careers beyond college or international competition. The league opened doors for players to pursue hockey at a professional level, offering a space to display their talents and inspire the next generation of female hockey players. This development was crucial not only for the players but also for the growth of the sport, as it provided young girls with role models and a clear pathway to pursue hockey professionally.

The establishment of the NWHL was met with enthusiasm and support from the hockey community, including fans, players, and sponsors. It represented a major stride in the journey towards equality in sports, challenging the status quo and redefining the landscape of professional hockey. The league's formation was a bold statement about the value and potential of women's hockey, and it set the stage for continued growth and development of the sport. The NWHL's founding has had a lasting impact, contributing significantly to the visibility and viability of women's hockey as a professional sport.

Challenges Faced

The early years of the National Women's Hockey League (NWHL) were fraught with a variety of challenges, ranging from financial constraints to logistical hurdles and societal barriers. As a pioneering venture in professional women's hockey, the NWHL had to navigate a landscape that was largely uncharted and, at times, unwelcoming. One of the most pressing challenges was financial sustainability. Securing adequate funding and sponsorship was a constant battle. Unlike well-established men's leagues, the NWHL did not have a significant influx of revenue from television deals or high-profile sponsors at its inception. The league had to be creative in its approach to generating income, relying heavily on ticket sales, merchandise, and smaller-scale sponsorships. This financial uncertainty impacted various aspects of the league, including player salaries, team operations, and overall growth.

Logistical challenges were also a significant hurdle. Organizing a new professional sports league involves a complex array of tasks, from scheduling games to ensuring suitable venues and managing travel arrangements. The NWHL had to coordinate these logistics while working within the constraints of a limited budget, which often meant finding cost-effective solutions without compromising the quality of the players' experience. Balancing these logistical demands while striving to maintain a high standard of professionalism was a continual challenge for the league's management.

Additionally, the NWHL faced societal challenges, particularly in terms of visibility and support. Women's sports historically have received less media coverage and public attention compared to men's sports. The NWHL had to work tirelessly to gain media exposure and build a fan base. This effort involved not just marketing and promotion but also battling entrenched societal perceptions about women's sports. The league had to convince potential fans, sponsors, and media outlets that women's hockey was worth watching and supporting.

Despite these obstacles, the NWHL persisted, driven by a commitment to growing women's hockey and providing professional opportunities for female athletes. The league's early years were a testament to resilience and determination in the face of significant challenges. The NWHL's efforts to overcome financial, logistical, and societal barriers laid a foundation for the future growth and success of the league. These challenges, while daunting, also served as catalysts for innovation and progress, pushing the league to find creative solutions and forge new paths in the world of professional women's hockey.

Significant Milestones

Throughout its history, the National Women's Hockey League (NWHL) has achieved several significant milestones that have contributed to its growth and prominence in the world of professional sports. These milestones are not just markers of progress but also reflections of the league's dedication to advancing women's hockey. One of the key milestones in the NWHL's history was the signing of its first major sponsorship deal. This sponsorship was a crucial step in establishing the league's credibility and financial stability. It signaled to the broader sports community that women's hockey was a viable and valuable market. The backing of a major sponsor provided the league with much-needed resources and helped to increase its visibility.

Another notable milestone was the NWHL's first nationally televised game. This broadcast was a significant achievement in terms of media exposure and represented a breakthrough in bringing women's hockey to a wider audience. The televised game not only showcased the high level of competition in the league but also brought the excitement and talent of NWHL players into the homes of sports fans across the country. This increased exposure was instrumental in attracting new fans and sponsors to the league.

The NWHL has also formed several important partnerships throughout its history. These partnerships, with various organizations and entities, have been vital in expanding the league's reach and impact. From collaborations with youth hockey programs to partnerships with equipment manufacturers and other professional sports teams, these alliances have provided the NWHL with additional resources and opportunities to promote the league and its players.

Additionally, the NWHL has reached milestones in terms of expansion. The addition of new teams to the league has been a key factor in its growth. Expanding the league's footprint has not only increased the level of competition but also brought professional women's hockey to new markets. This expansion has been fundamental in building a broader fan base and providing more opportunities for female hockey players to compete at a professional level.

These milestones represent more than just achievements in the league's timeline; they are indicative of the NWHL's ongoing efforts to promote and elevate women's hockey. Each milestone has played a part in shaping the league and has contributed to its mission of providing a platform for female athletes to showcase their talents and passion for the sport. The NWHL's history is marked by these significant moments, each a step forward in the league's journey toward greater recognition and success.

Impact on Women's Hockey

The National Women's Hockey League (NWHL) has had a profound impact on the advancement of women's hockey, influencing various aspects of the sport from the grassroots to the professional level. The creation of the NWHL marked a significant step in providing female athletes with professional opportunities in hockey, a sport where such opportunities were previously limited. By establishing a professional league for women, the NWHL has not only given elite female hockey players a platform to continue their careers after college or international play but has also set a new standard for the sport. The presence of a professional league has been crucial in legitimizing women's hockey as a career path, encouraging more women to pursue the sport at a high level.

The NWHL's influence extends to youth participation in hockey. The league's players serve as role models for young girls who aspire to play hockey, demonstrating that there is a future in the sport beyond amateur levels. The visibility of female hockey players in a professional setting has inspired a new generation of young girls to lace up skates and hit the ice. The NWHL has actively engaged in community outreach and youth development programs, further fostering interest and participation in women's hockey. These initiatives not only promote the sport but also empower young girls, showing them the possibilities within hockey.

Internationally, the NWHL has played a role in increasing the visibility of women's hockey. By providing a platform for top female hockey players from around the world to showcase their skills, the league has contributed to the global recognition of the sport. The presence of international players in the NWHL has also facilitated cross-cultural exchange and learning, enriching the experience for both players and fans. This international aspect has helped to raise the standard of play and competitiveness in the league, contributing to the overall growth of women's hockey worldwide.

Moreover, the NWHL has been instrumental in advocating for better conditions and more opportunities for female athletes in hockey. From pushing for fair pay to ensuring better facilities and resources, the league's efforts have highlighted the need for equality in sports. The NWHL's existence challenges the status quo and pushes the boundaries of what is possible for women in hockey, setting a precedent for other sports to follow. The league's impact on women's hockey is multifaceted, encompassing the development of the sport at the grassroots level, providing opportunities for professional growth, and enhancing the visibility and status of women's hockey on the international stage. The NWHL's role in advancing women's hockey has been transformative, paving the way for future generations of female athletes and contributing to the ongoing evolution of the sport.

LeBron James: From High School Phenom to NBA Superstar

Early Years and High School Fame

LeBron James' journey from a high school basketball prodigy to an NBA superstar is a tale of talent, hard work, and meteoric rise to fame. Born on December 30, 1984, in Akron, Ohio, LeBron's early life was filled with challenges, including financial instability and frequent moves. However, basketball became a stabilizing and central part of his life from a young age. His immense talent was evident early on and he quickly made a name for himself in the local basketball circuits.

LeBron attended St. Vincent-St. Mary High School in Akron, where he became a national sensation for his extraordinary basketball skills. His high school career was nothing short of phenomenal, marked by numerous accolades and widespread media attention. LeBron led his team to three state championships in four years, showcasing his ability to dominate games with his scoring, passing, and defensive prowess. His high school games began to attract large crowds and national media coverage, an unusual phenomenon for high school sports at the time.

LeBron's high school fame was not limited to his on-court performances. He was featured on the cover of "Sports Illustrated" magazine as a junior, with the title "The Chosen One," signaling his potential to be one of the greats in basketball. This level of attention and hype around a high school player was unprecedented, and LeBron was at the center of intense scrutiny and expectation. Despite this pressure, he continued to excel and improve, drawing comparisons to some of the greatest basketball players of all time.

LeBron's high school years were instrumental in shaping his future career. They were a period of growth, both as a player and as a person, under the intense glare of the national spotlight. His performances on the high school stage set the foundation for his future success and paved the way for his entry into the NBA. LeBron's early years and high school fame are evidence of his exceptional talent and his ability to handle the pressures of being in the public eye from a young age. His journey from a high school phenom to an NBA superstar began in the gyms of Akron, where he first displayed the talent and work ethic that would make him one of the most influential athletes in the world.

NBA Draft and Rookie Season

LeBron James' entry into the NBA was as momentous as his high school career, marked by anticipation and excitement. In the 2003 NBA Draft, he was selected as the first overall pick by the Cleveland Cavaliers, a choice that was widely anticipated given his phenomenal talent and potential. LeBron's selection was significant not only for him personally but also for the Cavaliers, who were gaining a player already known as a once-in-a-generation talent. The 2003 draft itself was renowned for its depth of talent, with LeBron being part of a draft class that included other future NBA stars.

LeBron's transition to the NBA was highly scrutinized, with many wondering if he could live up to the lofty expectations set by his high school career. Any doubts, however, were quickly dispelled as he began his rookie season. LeBron made an immediate impact in the league, showcasing a level of skill and maturity that was extraordinary for a player straight out of high school. His debut game against the Sacramento Kings was a glimpse of what was to come; he scored 25 points, setting the record for the most points scored by a prep-to-pro player in his debut performance.

Throughout his rookie season, LeBron continued to impress both fans and critics. He demonstrated a well-rounded game, excelling in scoring, assists, and rebounds. His ability to impact the game in multiple ways and his basketball IQ were evident from the start. LeBron's performances were not just statistically impressive; they were also critical in improving the Cavaliers' competitiveness in the league. His presence brought a new energy to the team and reinvigorated the fan base.

The culmination of LeBron's remarkable rookie season was his winning of the NBA Rookie of the Year Award. This achievement was a testament to his hard work, talent, and the successful transition he had made from high school to professional basketball. LeBron finished his rookie season with averages of 20.9 points, 5.5 rebounds, and 5.9 assists per game, joining the likes of Michael Jordan and Oscar Robertson as the only players in NBA history to average at least 20 points, five rebounds, and five assists per game in their rookie season.

LeBron's draft into the NBA and his subsequent rookie season marked the beginning of what would become one of the most illustrious careers in basketball history. His ability to meet and exceed expectations, even under the immense pressure of being the first overall pick, set the stage for his future success in the league. LeBron's journey from a high school phenom to a successful NBA rookie showcased his extraordinary talent and his readiness to take on the challenges of professional basketball.

Championships and MVP Awards

LeBron James' NBA career, marked by extraordinary achievements, reached new heights with his multiple NBA championships and MVP awards. These accolades not only underscored his individual brilliance but also his impact on team success. LeBron's journey to NBA championships began with a significant decision in 2010 to join the Miami Heat, forming a star-studded team alongside Dwyane Wade and Chris Bosh. This move was a turning point in his career and shifted the landscape of the NBA.

With the Miami Heat, LeBron's pursuit of an NBA championship was realized. He won his first NBA title in 2012, a momentous achievement that solidified his status as one of the game's greats. The Heat, under LeBron's leadership, defeated the Oklahoma City Thunder in the Finals. LeBron's performance throughout the season and the playoffs was exceptional, earning him the NBA Finals MVP award. He followed this up with another championship in 2013, where the Heat successfully defended their title against the San Antonio Spurs. LeBron once again was pivotal in the Finals, showcasing his versatility, basketball IQ, and clutch performances.

LeBron's return to the Cleveland Cavaliers in 2014 marked another significant chapter in his career. His decision to return to his home state was driven by a desire to bring a championship to

Cleveland. This dream was realized in 2016, in what is considered one of the greatest comebacks in NBA Finals history. The Cavaliers, led by LeBron, overcame a 3-1 deficit to defeat the Golden State Warriors. LeBron's performance in the series was historic and he was unanimously named Finals MVP, becoming the third player in NBA history to record a triple-double in a Finals Game 7.

In addition to his championships, LeBron has been recognized as the NBA's Most Valuable Player (MVP) four times (2009, 2010, 2012, 2013). These awards were evidence of his all-around excellence and his ability to elevate the performance of his teams. LeBron's MVP seasons were characterized by his dominance on both ends of the floor, his exceptional passing and scoring ability, and his leadership on and off the court.

LeBron's NBA championships and MVP awards are not just milestones in his career; they are reflections of his evolution as a player and his impact on the sport. His championships with both Miami and Cleveland showcased his ability to lead and excel in different team environments. Meanwhile, his MVP awards are indicative of his consistent excellence throughout his career and his status as one of the best players in the league. LeBron's achievements in winning multiple championships and MVP awards have solidified his legacy as one of the greatest basketball players of all time, a player who has left an indelible mark on the NBA.

Off-Court Impact

LeBron James' influence extends far beyond the basketball court, with his off-court endeavors, particularly in philanthropy, highlighting his commitment to making a positive impact in the community. One of the most significant of these endeavors is the establishment of the I PROMISE School in his hometown of Akron, Ohio. This public school, a collaboration between the

LeBron James Family Foundation and Akron Public Schools, opened in 2018 and is designed to serve at-risk children by providing them with a stable and supportive learning environment.

The I PROMISE School is unique in its approach to education, focusing on the comprehensive needs of its students. It offers smaller class sizes, a longer school day, and a longer school year, aiming to provide more learning opportunities for the students. The curriculum is designed to be both rigorous and engaging, with a strong emphasis on science, technology, engineering, and mathematics (STEM) subjects, along with a focus on developing critical thinking and problem-solving skills.

Beyond the academic aspects, the I PROMISE School provides resources to address the social and emotional needs of its students. This includes a family resource center, which offers support for parents and families, including job placement assistance and legal aid. The school also provides free meals, uniforms, and transportation to students, alleviating some of the common barriers to education that students from disadvantaged backgrounds face.

LeBron's philanthropic work with the I PROMISE School is part of a broader commitment to giving back to his community. His foundation has been involved in various initiatives aimed at helping children and families in Akron. These initiatives include providing college scholarships, renovating community centers, and hosting annual events like bike-a-thons and Thanksgiving dinners for families in need.

LeBron's off-court impact through his philanthropic efforts speaks volumes about his character and his dedication to creating positive change. His investment in the I PROMISE School and other community initiatives reflects his understanding of the broader role he can play in society as a public figure and athlete. Through his actions, LeBron has shown a commitment to using his platform and resources to empower those in underprivileged communities, setting an example of how athletes can meaningfully contribute to social change. His work off the court, particularly with the I PROMISE School, is a testament to his belief in the power of education to transform lives and communities.

The Legend of Michael Jordan

Early Challenges and College Success

Michael Jordan's path to becoming a basketball legend was not without its initial setbacks and challenges, which played a crucial role in shaping his storied career. One of the most well-known anecdotes from Jordan's early life is his failure to make the varsity basketball team during his sophomore year at Emsley A. Laney High School in Wilmington, North Carolina. This rejection, often cited as a pivotal moment in Jordan's life, fueled his determination to succeed and become a better player. He used this setback as motivation, dedicating himself to rigorous practice and improvement. The following year, he made the varsity team and quickly established himself as a standout player, showcasing his talent and work ethic.

Jordan's high school success led to a scholarship at the University of North Carolina (UNC) at Chapel Hill, where he played under legendary coach Dean Smith. At UNC, Jordan's skills continued to flourish. He was named ACC Freshman of the Year in 1982, showcasing his immediate impact on the team. His time at UNC was marked by significant growth, both as a player and as a team contributor. Jordan was known for his scoring ability, defensive prowess, and his capacity to play under pressure – traits that would become hallmarks of his professional career.

The crowning moment of Jordan's college career came in the 1982 NCAA Championship game against Georgetown University. In a closely contested game, with UNC trailing by one point, Jordan made the iconic game-winning jump shot with just 17 seconds left on the clock. This shot is not only remembered as the highlight of the 1982 NCAA Tournament but also as a defining moment in Jordan's career, symbolizing his clutch performance under pressure and his emergence as a top player. It was a precursor to the numerous game-winning shots and clutch performances that would define his career in the NBA.

Jordan's early challenges, followed by his college success and the iconic shot to win the 1982 NCAA Championship, laid the foundation for his ascent to basketball immortality. These experiences at Laney High School and UNC shaped his competitive spirit, his relentless pursuit of excellence, and his ability to rise to the occasion when it mattered most. This early period of Jordan's life and career is a reflection of his resilience and determination, qualities that would propel him to become one of the greatest athletes in the history of sports.

NBA Domination and First Retirement

Michael Jordan's entry into the NBA began with the Chicago Bulls drafting him third overall in the 1984 NBA Draft, a decision that would dramatically alter the franchise's destiny and the landscape of the league. Jordan's impact was immediate and profound; he finished his rookie season with an average of 28.2 points per game and earned the NBA Rookie of the Year Award. His remarkable athleticism, scoring ability, and competitive drive quickly turned him into one of the most exciting players to watch in the league.

As Jordan's career progressed with the Bulls, he evolved from a high-scoring guard into the face of the NBA. His ability to dominate games, coupled with his flair for dramatic, high-flying plays, made him a favorite among fans and a nightmare for opponents. Jordan led the league in scoring for seven consecutive seasons from 1986 to 1993, highlighting his offensive prowess and ability to consistently perform at an elite level.

The pinnacle of Jordan's career with the Bulls came in the form of the team's first three-peat of NBA championships from 1991 to 1993. These championship victories were not just a testament to Jordan's individual brilliance but also his ability to elevate the play of his teammates. The first championship in 1991 was particularly significant as it established the Bulls as a powerhouse in the NBA and provided Jordan with his long-sought validation as a winner. The 1992 and 1993 championships further cemented the Bulls' dominance in the league and Jordan's status as the game's premier player.

In a move that shocked the sports world, Michael Jordan announced his first retirement from basketball in October 1993. This decision came at the height of his career, following his father's tragic death and amidst growing pressures and scrutiny in his professional life. Jordan's retirement sent ripples through the NBA, as he had become synonymous with the sport. His departure from basketball was a significant moment, marking the end of a dominant era for the Bulls and leaving fans and players alike wondering what the future held for both Jordan and the league.

Jordan's first retirement from the NBA marked the end of a chapter characterized by individual accolades, team success, and a transformative impact on the sport. His rise to superstardom with the Bulls and the subsequent three-peat of championships had elevated him to an iconic status, while his sudden retirement added an unexpected twist to an already legendary career. This period of Jordan's life encapsulates his journey from a promising young talent to a global sports icon and the abrupt pause that left the basketball world in anticipation of his next move.

Baseball Career and NBA Comeback

Michael Jordan's foray into professional baseball following his first retirement from the NBA was an unexpected turn in his sporting journey. In February 1994, Jordan signed a minor league baseball contract with the Chicago White Sox, an affiliate of the Birmingham Barons. His decision to switch sports was influenced by a childhood dream and his father's love for baseball. While Jordan's baseball career was met with mixed reactions and varying degrees of success, it showcased his willingness to challenge himself and step out of his comfort zone.

During his time with the Barons, Jordan displayed commendable effort and a strong work ethic, but it became clear that his prowess on the baseball field did not match his basketball dominance. He played as an outfielder and had a batting average of .202, with 3 home runs, 51 RBIs, and 30 stolen bases. Despite not reaching the same heights in baseball as he did in basketball, Jordan's stint in the sport demonstrated his competitive spirit and his dedication to pursuing his personal goals.

Jordan's return to the NBA in March 1995 marked the beginning of another extraordinary chapter in his basketball career. Announcing his comeback with a famous two-word press release, "I'm back," Jordan rejoined the Chicago Bulls towards the end of the 1994-1995 season. His return reignited excitement in the NBA and fans eagerly anticipated his return to the court. While the Bulls were eliminated in the playoffs that season, it set the stage for what would be another remarkable run of success.

The 1995-1996 season marked the start of the Bulls' second three-peat of championships, with Jordan at the forefront. He led the Bulls to an NBA record 72 wins during the regular season and was named the league's Most Valuable Player. The Bulls dominated the playoffs and won the NBA championship, a triumphant return for Jordan. The subsequent two seasons, 1996-1997 and 1997-1998, saw the Bulls continue their dominance, winning two more championships and solidifying their legacy as one of the greatest teams in NBA history.

Jordan's comeback to the NBA and the Bulls' second three-peat symbolized his resilience, determination, and enduring skill. His brief baseball career and subsequent return to basketball highlight a period in his life characterized by personal challenges, a pursuit of dreams, and a triumphant return to the pinnacle of his sport. This phase of Jordan's career further cemented his status as not just a basketball legend, but a global sports icon known for his remarkable ability to succeed, adapt, and excel in the face of new challenges.

Legacy and Cultural Impact

Michael Jordan's legacy as one of the greatest basketball players of all time is undisputed and his influence extends far beyond the basketball court into popular culture and the business world. Jordan's impact on the game of basketball is monumental; he revolutionized the sport with his extraordinary talent, competitive spirit, and his ability to perform under pressure. His six NBA championships and five MVP awards speak to his dominance, but his influence is also measured in how he changed the perception of basketball players as global icons.

Jordan's cultural impact is as significant as his athletic achievements. He became a cultural icon, transcending sports and becoming a household name around the world. His partnership with Nike and the creation of the Air Jordan brand revolutionized sports marketing and the sneaker industry. The Air Jordan brand became a symbol of style, performance, and excellence, and it continues to be a dominant force in the market. Jordan's influence in fashion, particularly in the realm of athletic wear, is profound and enduring.

In popular culture, Michael Jordan became a figure of inspiration and admiration. He was the subject of numerous endorsements and television appearances, and even led the cast of the movie "Space Jam," which blended the worlds of basketball and entertainment. His competitive nature and dedication to excellence made him a role model for athletes and non-athletes alike. Jordan's story of overcoming challenges, striving for greatness, and achieving his dreams resonates with people of different ages and backgrounds.

Beyond his playing days, Jordan's influence in the sport and business of basketball continues. He became the first former NBA player to become the majority owner of a league franchise, the Charlotte Hornets. His involvement in team ownership and management demonstrates his ongoing commitment to the sport and his desire to impact the game from a different perspective. Jordan's voice and opinion in the realm of basketball and sports, in general, carry significant weight, highlighting his enduring presence in the industry.

Michael Jordan's legacy is multifaceted. As a player, he was a relentless competitor and a winner. As a cultural icon, he is a symbol of excellence and global recognition. In the business world, he is an innovator and a trailblazer. His impact on basketball, popular culture, and the business of sports is profound and lasting. Jordan's journey from a high school player who was cut from his team to becoming a global icon is a story of determination, talent, and the relentless pursuit of greatness. His legacy continues to inspire and influence, making him a permanent fixture in the annals of sports history and beyond.

Cristiano Ronaldo's Work Ethic

Early Years and Sporting Lisbon

Cristiano Ronaldo, one of football's most illustrious figures, is as much celebrated for his extraordinary work ethic as he is for his on-field brilliance. This relentless drive, which became the cornerstone of his career, was nurtured early in his life in Portugal and during his formative years at Sporting Lisbon.

Humble Beginnings in Madeira

Cristiano Ronaldo dos Santos Aveiro was born on February 5, 1985, in Funchal, Madeira, Portugal. Growing up in a working-class neighborhood, Ronaldo's early life was far from luxurious. His family faced financial hardships, but these challenges laid the foundation for his character – instilling a sense of determination and the importance of hard work.

From a very young age, Ronaldo showed a deep passion for football. His talent was evident, but it was his work ethic that truly set him apart. He would spend hours practicing, often skipping meals or sacrificing leisure time to hone his skills. His dedication to improving himself, even as a child, was a precursor to the discipline and commitment that would later define his professional career.

Joining Sporting Lisbon

Ronaldo's journey took a significant turn when he joined Sporting Lisbon, one of Portugal's most prestigious football academies, at the age of just 12. Moving away from his family to Lisbon was a challenging step for the young Ronaldo, but it was a sacrifice he was willing to make to pursue his dream of becoming a professional footballer.

At Sporting Lisbon, Ronaldo's work ethic intensified. He was known for being the first to arrive at training and the last to leave, constantly working on his technique, fitness, and understanding of the game. His desire to improve was relentless; he would often request extra training sessions to work on his weaknesses, showcasing an extraordinary level of dedication for someone so young.

Development of His Work Ethic

It was during his time at Sporting Lisbon that Ronaldo's work ethic began to truly develop. He recognized early on that talent alone was not enough to succeed at the highest level. His commitment to training, his focus on physical conditioning, and his determination to be the best were evident. Ronaldo was not just working hard; he was working smart, focusing on all aspects of his game.

His coaches at Sporting Lisbon were instrumental in nurturing his work ethic. They provided the guidance and structure he needed to channel his efforts effectively. Ronaldo's attitude towards training and improvement impressed everyone at the club. He was not content with being good; he wanted to be the best, and he was willing to put in the work to get there.

Early Signs of Future Greatness

Ronaldo's time at Sporting Lisbon laid the groundwork for what would become an extraordinary career. His performances for the youth teams were a glimpse of his potential, and he quickly progressed through the ranks. His debut for the Sporting Lisbon senior team at the age of 17 was a testament to his talent and hard work.

Ronaldo's early years in Portugal and his time at Sporting Lisbon were key in the development of his work ethic. From the streets of Madeira to the training grounds of Lisbon, Ronaldo's journey was marked by an unwavering commitment to excellence. This period of his life was not just about developing his skills as a footballer; it was about instilling a mindset – a relentless drive to improve, to succeed, and to defy the odds.

Success at Manchester United and Real Madrid

Manchester United: The Making of a Superstar

Ronaldo's transfer to Manchester United in 2003 was a significant moment in his career. Under the guidance of Sir Alex Ferguson, Ronaldo transformed from a talented teenager into one of the world's best footballers. His time at United was characterized by rigorous training, a relentless drive to improve, and a determination to succeed at the highest level.

During his six years at Manchester United, Ronaldo's work ethic became legendary. He was known for staying after training sessions to work on his free-kicks, improve his dribbling, and enhance his physical strength. His dedication to self-improvement was evident in his evolution as a player. He developed into a formidable goal-scorer, a master of aerial duels, and a player capable of single-handedly changing the course of games.

Ronaldo's impact at United was profound. He helped the club to three consecutive Premier League titles (2007, 2008, and 2009), the FA Cup, two League Cups, and the UEFA Champions League in 2008. Individually, he garnered numerous accolades, including the Ballon d'Or in 2008. His final season with United was particularly remarkable, where he scored 42 goals in all competitions, showcasing his transformation into one of the most lethal forwards in the game.

Real Madrid: Scaling New Heights

Ronaldo's move to Real Madrid in 2009 for a then-world record transfer fee was the start of a new chapter. At Madrid, his work ethic intensified as he strived to leave his mark in one of the world's most prestigious clubs. Ronaldo's training regime, discipline, and dedication to maintaining peak physical condition were unparalleled. He continuously worked on refining his skills, adapting his style of play, and pushing the limits of his physical abilities.

At Real Madrid, Ronaldo's goal-scoring record was nothing short of phenomenal. He became the club's all-time top scorer in just six seasons, an achievement that speaks volumes about his  consistency and dedication. Ronaldo was instrumental in Real Madrid's dominance in Europe, contributing significantly to their four UEFA Champions League titles during his tenure (2014, 2016, 2017, and 2018).

His performances in Madrid were characterized by remarkable athleticism, tactical intelligence, and a hunger for goals. Ronaldo evolved his game to become more of a central striker, utilizing his aerial prowess, positional sense, and lethal finishing. His impact went beyond individual accolades; he was a leader on the pitch, driving his team to numerous victories and titles.

Legacy of Dedication and Excellence

Ronaldo's stints at Manchester United and Real Madrid are testament to his extraordinary work ethic and pursuit of excellence. He set new standards in professional football, not only in terms of skill and talent but also in terms of dedication and discipline. His relentless drive to improve, to adapt, and to succeed at the highest levels of football has inspired a generation of players.

Maintaining Peak Performance

Cristiano Ronaldo's sustained success at the pinnacle of world football is a reflection not only to his natural talent but more significantly to his unwavering commitment to training, fitness, and maintaining peak performance levels. Ronaldo's approach to his physical and mental preparation is as disciplined and methodical as it is extraordinary, setting him apart even among the elite athletes in the sport.

Training Regimen and Discipline

Ronaldo's training regimen is the cornerstone of his footballing longevity and success. He is known for his rigorous and meticulously planned workouts, both on and off the field. At the club level, Ronaldo often engages in additional training sessions beyond the team's regular practices, focusing on enhancing his strength, speed, and agility. His training regime includes a mix of high-intensity drills, technical skills work, cardiovascular exercises, and targeted strength training to improve his overall athleticism and footballing abilities.

His discipline extends to all aspects of his fitness regime. Ronaldo is known for his strict diet, which is carefully tailored to optimize his physical condition and performance levels. He pays close attention to his nutrition, hydration, and rest, understanding that these are as crucial to performance as the training itself. This holistic approach to fitness and wellness has been a key factor in his ability to perform at the highest level consistently.

Physical Attributes and Adaptation

One of the most striking aspects of Ronaldo's career has been his physical transformation and adaptation. He entered the professional football scene as a slender teenager with incredible agility and speed. Over the years, he has transformed his physique into that of a powerful athlete, capable of competing against the most robust defenders. This physical evolution is a direct result of his commitment to a rigorous fitness regime, focusing on building muscle strength, endurance, and explosive power.

Ronaldo's ability to adapt his style of play with his changing physical attributes is equally noteworthy. As he matured, he transitioned from a fleet-footed winger to a prolific striker, altering his game to maximize his efficiency and effectiveness on the field. This adaptability has extended his career and maintained his status as one of the best in the game, even as he navigated different phases of his physical peak.

Mental Strength and Professionalism

Ronaldo's approach to maintaining peak performance is not limited to physical training and nutrition; it also encompasses a strong mental attitude. His mental fortitude, focus, and professionalism are integral components of his success. Ronaldo approaches each training session, each game, and each season with a relentless desire to improve and succeed. His competitive nature drives him to push his limits continually.

His professionalism in managing his career is exemplary. Ronaldo is meticulous about his recovery processes, understanding the importance of rest and recuperation in a demanding sport like football. He utilizes a combination of rest, physiotherapy, and modern recovery technologies to stay in optimal shape.

Influence and Inspiration

Cristiano Ronaldo's commitment to maintaining peak performance has set a new benchmark in professional sports. He has redefined what it means to be a professional athlete in terms of preparation, training, and longevity. His example serves as an inspiration to aspiring athletes, illustrating that talent, while crucial, must be coupled with hard work, discipline, and a relentless pursuit of excellence.

Role Model and Legacy

Ronaldo as a Role Model

Ronaldo's journey from a humble background in Madeira to becoming one of the world's greatest footballers is a source of inspiration for many. He epitomizes the idea that with enough hard work and determination, one can overcome any obstacle and achieve their dreams. His dedication to training, fitness, and constant improvement makes him an ideal role model for young athletes in football and beyond.

His meticulous approach to his career - from diet and training to mental preparation and recovery - shows a level of professionalism and dedication that is rarely seen. Ronaldo does not rely solely on his natural talent; instead, he complements it with a rigorous work ethic. This message, that success is a result of hard work as much as talent, resonates with young athletes striving to reach the top of their sports.

Influence on Young Players

Ronaldo's influence extends beyond his fan base to impact young players across the globe. Many emerging footballers look up to him, not just for his skills and achievements on the field but for his discipline and attitude towards the game. His focus on continuous improvement, setting personal goals, and relentless drive to win has set a benchmark for aspiring footballers.

In training facilities and academies worldwide, Ronaldo's routines and training methods are often emulated. His impact is such that he has redefined what it means to be a professional athlete in terms of physical preparation and longevity in the sport.

Legacy in Football

Ronaldo's legacy in football is multi-dimensional. On the field, he will be remembered as one of the greatest ever, with numerous records, titles, and personal accolades. Off the field, his legacy will be defined by his professionalism, work ethic, and the way he has conducted his career.

Throughout his tenure in clubs like Manchester United, Real Madrid, and Juventus, Ronaldo has consistently pushed the boundaries of what is possible, both in terms of individual performance and team success. His influence in these clubs goes beyond the goals and the trophies; he has been a leader and a motivator, elevating the standards of those around him.

Ronaldo's Broader Impact

Beyond the realm of football, Ronaldo has become a cultural icon, known for his philanthropic efforts and his role as a global ambassador for various causes. His journey is a testament to the power of sports as a tool for positive change, both in an individual's life and in the broader community.

Cristiano Ronaldo's work ethic and career trajectory have made him a role model for millions around the world. His legacy in football will be remembered for his incredible achievements and for the exemplary determination and discipline he demonstrated throughout his career. Ronaldo has shown that while talent can get you far, it is hard work, dedication, and a constant pursuit of excellence that truly define a sporting legend. As aspiring athletes look to him for inspiration, Ronaldo's legacy continues to grow, influencing and shaping the future of football and sports in general.

Lionel Messi's Perseverance

Early Challenges in Rosario, Argentina

Lionel Andrés Messi was born on June 24, 1987, in Rosario, Argentina, to Jorge Messi, a steel factory manager, and his wife Celia Cuccittini, who worked in a magnet manufacturing workshop. Raised in a football-loving family, Messi developed a passion for the game at a very young age. He was greatly influenced by his family, especially his maternal grandmother, Celia, who accompanied him to training and matches. Messi joined his first soccer club, Grandoli, at the age of four, where his father coached him.

The young Messi was always smaller than his peers, a trait that would become a significant challenge in his burgeoning football career. Despite his diminutive stature, his talent was undeniable. He moved to Newell's Old Boys, a local club in Rosario, at the age of eight. His skills on the pitch were extraordinary, showcasing remarkable dribbling ability, vision, and natural football intelligence. Messi was part of a local youth team nicknamed "The Machine of '87," known for their unbeatable record and incredible talent.

Battling Growth Hormone Deficiency

At the age of 10, Messi faced a major obstacle that threatened to derail his dreams of becoming a professional footballer. He was diagnosed with a growth hormone deficiency, a condition that required expensive medical treatment, including regular injections. The cost of the treatment was beyond the financial means of the Messi family.

Despite this setback, Messi's determination and passion for the game did not wane. His family was committed to finding a way to support his treatment and continue his football development. This period was one of uncertainty and hardship for Messi and his family, as they searched for solutions to ensure he could receive the necessary treatment and pursue his football aspirations.

The Move to Barcelona

Messi's talent caught the attention of FC Barcelona's scouts when he was just 13 years old. Carles Rexach, the sporting director of Barcelona at the time, saw something special in the young Argentine and was willing to take a chance on him. In a now-legendary decision, Rexach offered Messi a contract written on a napkin – an agreement to bring him to Barcelona's famed youth academy, La Masia, and to cover his medical treatment.

The move to Barcelona was a life-changing moment for Messi. Uprooting his life and moving to Spain was a significant challenge, particularly at such a young age. He left behind his friends, family, and familiar surroundings to embark on a journey in a new country, with a new language and culture. The transition was difficult; Messi was initially homesick and struggled to integrate into his new environment. However, his talent shone through. At La Masia, Messi's skills developed rapidly, and he quickly adapted to the style of play, exceeding expectations at every level of the youth system.

Rise to Stardom

Early Years at La Masia

Messi's journey at La Masia, Barcelona's youth academy, began in 2000 when he was just 13 years old. Moving to a new country and adapting to a new culture was challenging, but Messi's focus remained unwaveringly on soccer. At La Masia, he found himself in an environment that prized technical skill, tactical understanding, and a deep love for the game – all elements that resonated with Messi's natural style of play.

In these formative years, Messi underwent not only physical development, courtesy of his treatment for growth hormone deficiency, but also significant soccer development. Under the tutelage of some of the best youth coaches, he honed his skills, particularly his incredible dribbling ability, close ball control, and vision on the field. Messi's growth as a player was rapid, and he quickly moved through the ranks of the youth teams.

His performances in youth matches were nothing short of phenomenal. Messi consistently played against older and physically larger opponents, yet his talent shone through. He became known for changing games single-handedly, utilizing his low center of gravity to maneuver past defenders with ease.

Breaking Records in Youth Leagues

Messi's time in Barcelona's youth teams was marked by record-breaking performances. He was not just another promising young player; he was a prodigy setting new standards in youth soccer. His goal-scoring record was particularly impressive, often scoring upwards of 40 goals in a season for various youth teams. These extraordinary feats were early indicators of the impact Messi would have on the world of soccer.

Transition to the First Team

Messi's transition to Barcelona's first team was a natural progression given his astounding performances at the youth level. His first-team debut came at the age of 16 in a friendly match against FC Porto in November 2003. This was a significant moment, marking his entry into professional soccer.

In October 2004, at just 17, Messi made his official competitive debut for Barcelona against Espanyol. This match marked his entry into the record books as the youngest player to play in an official match for Barcelona at that time. His first league goal came the following year, against Albacete, making him the youngest scorer for the club in a La Liga match.

Establishing Himself in the First Team

Messi's integration into the first team was seamless, thanks to the nurturing environment at La Masia and his extraordinary talent. Under the guidance of coaches like Frank Rijkaard and later Pep Guardiola, Messi evolved from a talented youngster to a key player for the team.

His early years in the first team were marked by dazzling performances, showcasing not just his goal-scoring ability but also his capacity to create opportunities and assist his teammates. Messi's playing style, characterized by close ball control, rapid dribbling, and an uncanny ability to find spaces in the defense, fit perfectly with Barcelona's style of play.

Messi's breakthrough season came in 2006-2007, where he scored 14 goals in 26 league games and produced numerous assists. He played a crucial role in Barcelona's domestic and European campaigns, displaying a level of maturity and skill that belied his age. It was during this season that comparisons with soccer legends like Diego Maradona began to surface, not just for his style of play but for his impact on the game.

Rising to International Acclaim

Messi's rise to stardom at Barcelona was not just about his on-field performances. He became an integral part of a team that would go on to achieve tremendous success, both in Spain and internationally. His partnership with players like Xavi Hernandez and Andrés Iniesta was pivotal in Barcelona's dominance of European soccer.

By the time he was in his early twenties, Messi had already established himself as one of the world's best players. His consistent performances, incredible skill, and ability to produce moments of magic on the soccer field had earned him international acclaim. He was not just a star at Barcelona; he was a global soccer phenomenon, drawing attention and admiration from fans and players worldwide.

Career Highlights

Barcelona Triumphs and Records

At Barcelona, Messi's career is a chronicle of unprecedented success and record-setting performances. He became the backbone of a team that dominated both Spanish and European football for over a decade. One of the key highlights was Barcelona's treble win (La Liga, Copa del Rey, and UEFA Champions League) in the 2008-2009 season, a feat they repeated in the 2014-2015 season, with Messi playing a pivotal role in both triumphs.

Messi's scoring prowess saw him breaking multiple records. He is Barcelona's all-time top scorer and holds the record for the most goals in a calendar year, netting an astonishing 91 goals in 2012.

This record broke Gerd Müller's longstanding record of 85 goals in a calendar year. Messi also holds the record for the most hat-tricks in La Liga and the Champions League.

Another significant milestone has been his eight Ballon d'Or awards, the most by any player, which he won in 2009, 2010, 2011, 2012, 2015, 2019, 2021 and 2023. These awards are testament to his consistency and standing as the world's best player over different periods of his career.

Memorable Matches and Performances

Messi's career is studded with memorable matches that underscore his genius on the field. One of the most notable performances was against Real Madrid in the Champions League semi-finals in 2011, where he scored a mesmerizing solo goal, dribbling past several defenders before scoring. Another unforgettable moment was his hat-trick in the El Clásico against Real Madrid in 2007, announcing his arrival as a world-class talent.

In the 2014-2015 Champions League season, Messi produced a moment of magic against Bayern Munich in the semi-finals, leaving Jerome Boateng on the ground before chipping the ball over Manuel Neuer. These performances not only highlighted his individual brilliance but also his ability to rise to the occasion in crucial matches.

International Achievements with Argentina

On the international stage, Messi's journey with the Argentine national team has been a mix of individual brilliance and collective pursuit of glory. Despite early criticisms of his performance with the national team, Messi led Argentina to the finals of the 2014 FIFA World Cup, where they were narrowly defeated by Germany. His performance throughout the tournament earned him the Golden Ball as the tournament's best player.

One of Messi's most cherished career moments came in 2021 when he led Argentina to victory in the Copa América, his first major international trophy. His emotional response to this triumph was evidence of his deep connection with his national team and his relentless pursuit of success on the international stage.

Legacy and Influence

Messi's influence extends beyond his scoring records and individual accolades. He has redefined the perception of an ideal footballer with his unique style, combining incredible dribbling skills, vision, and playmaking abilities with prolific goal-scoring. He has been a role model for sportsmanship, consistently maintaining a high level of performance and professionalism throughout his career.

Messi's career highlights reflect a journey of extraordinary talent, unwavering dedication, and a relentless pursuit of greatness. His records and achievements with Barcelona and Argentina are testaments to his status as one of the greatest footballers of all time.

Personal Life and Legacy

Off-Field Persona

Away from the limelight of professional football, Messi is known for his reserved and humble nature. Despite his global fame, he has maintained a relatively private personal life. Messi married Antonela Roccuzzo, his childhood sweetheart, in 2017, in a ceremony that was both a celebration of their long-standing relationship and a rare glimpse into Messi's personal world. The couple has three sons, and Messi is often seen as a doting father, sharing moments with his family that portray a tender and grounded side, contrasting with his superstar status.

Messi's humility extends to his interactions with fans and in his conduct in the public eye. He is often described as unassuming and down-to-earth, qualities that endear him to fans and observers alike. This demeanor, combined with his extraordinary talent, has contributed to his widespread popularity and respect, transcending club rivalries and national loyalties.

Philanthropy and Social Responsibility

Messi's commitment to philanthropy is a significant aspect of his legacy. His dedication to charitable efforts is exemplified through the Leo Messi Foundation, established in 2007. The foundation focuses on access to education and health care for vulnerable children, reflecting Messi's deep concern for the well-being of children worldwide. It supports various projects, including the construction of schools, sports facilities, and children's hospitals, particularly in his home country, Argentina, as well as in other parts of the world.

One of the notable initiatives of his foundation is its collaboration with UNICEF, where Messi serves as a Goodwill Ambassador. Through this role, he has been involved in campaigns and projects aimed at improving the lives of children, particularly in areas affected by poverty, conflict, and disease. Messi's involvement in these efforts highlights his awareness of the global platform he possesses and his desire to use it for the betterment of society.

Influence on the Sport

Messi's influence on football is immeasurable. He has redefined what it means to be an attacking player, combining impeccable skill, vision, and consistency at the highest level of the game. His style of play, characterized by mesmerizing dribbling, acute footballing intelligence, and extraordinary goal-scoring ability, has inspired a new generation of footballers. Young players worldwide idolize him, aspiring to emulate his style and approach to the game.

Moreover, Messi has contributed to the global appeal of football. His rivalry with Cristiano Ronaldo, another footballing great of his era, has captivated fans and media, bringing heightened attention and excitement to the sport. Messi's career at Barcelona and his performances on the international stage with Argentina have contributed to the growth of football's popularity across different continents.

Legacy Beyond Football

Lionel Messi's legacy extends beyond his achievements on the football field. He embodies the ideals of sportsmanship, dedication, and humility, setting an example for athletes in all disciplines. His journey from a young boy facing significant health challenges in Rosario to becoming one of the greatest footballers in history is a story of perseverance and resilience. It is a narrative that resonates with people beyond football fans, inspiring them to overcome their challenges and pursue their dreams with dedication and humility.

References

Battista, Brianna. *Cristiano Ronaldo*. Rosen Publishing Group (2018)

Biography.com editors. Babe Ruth. Biography.com (2014). https://www.biography.com/athletes/babe-ruth. Accessed December 05, 2023.

Bishop, Chad. *A First for Fuller ... and for All*. Vu Commodores (2020). https://vucommodores.com/a-first-for-fuller-and-for-all/. Accessed November 28, 2023

Fanucchi, David. Miracle on Grass: How Hall of Famer Tommy Lasorda Led Team USA to a Shocking Upset Over Cuba, Capturing the Only Olympic Gold Medal in USA Baseball History. CreateSpace Independent Publishing Platform (2012).

Kottler, Dave. *HBYD BREAKDOWN: NWHL*. Hockey by Design (2021). http://hockeybydesign.com/2021/05/hbyd-breakdown-nwhl/. Accessed on December 05, 2023

Mendiola, Jordan. *The Complete Story of Tom Brady (The GOAT)*. Medium (2022). https://medium.com/long-term-perspective/the-complete-story-of-tom-brady-36cb0c89be41. Accessed December 02, 2023

Motin, Adam. The Legend of Michael Jordan, Triumph Books (2020)

Orr, Bobby. *Orr: My Story*. Penguin Canada (2013).

Perez, Mike. *Lionel Messi*. Welbeck Publishing Group Limited (2020).

The New York Times Editorial Staff. LeBron James. The New York Times Editorial Staff (2019).

Bonus: Free Book!

Are you ready to delve into the thrilling book in the series, absolutely free? Get ready to go deep into the world of yet another football legend! Just use your smartphone or tablet to scan the QR code below, then follow the simple prompts to receive the PDF.

www.ingramcontent.com/pod-product-compliance
Lightning Source LLC
Chambersburg PA
CBHW050206130526
44591CB00035B/2331